IF F

Greater Than a Tourist Book Series
Reviews from Readers

Good information to have to plan my trip to this destination.

-Pennie Farrell, Mexico

Great ideas for a port day.

-Mary Martin USA

Aptly titled, you won't just be a tourist after reading this book. You'll be greater than a tourist!

-Alan Warner, Grand Rapids, USA

Even though I only have three days to spend in San Miguel in an upcoming visit, I will use the author's suggestions to guide some of my time there. An easy read - with chapters named to guide me in directions I want to go.

-Robert Catapano, USA

Great insights from a local perspective! Useful information and a very good value!

-Sarah, USA

This series provides an in-depth experience through the eyes of a local. Reading these series will help you to travel the city in with confidence and it'll make your journey a unique one.

-Andrew Teoh, Ipoh, Malaysia

GREATER THAN A TOURIST- MANAMA BAHRAIN

50 Travel Tips from a Local

Mariel Diaz

Cover designed by: Ivana Stamenkovic
Cover Image: https://pixabay.com/en/muharraq-manama-bahrain-gulf-3439937/

Edited by:

CZYK Publishing Since 2011.

Greater Than a Tourist
Visit our website at www.GreaterThanaTourist.com

Lock Haven, PA
ISBN: 9781723984402

>TOURIST

50 TRAVEL TIPS FROM A LOCAL

BOOK DESCRIPTION

Are you excited about planning your next trip?

Do you want to try something new?

Would you like some guidance from a local?

If you answered yes to any of these questions, then this Greater Than a Tourist book is for you.

Greater Than a Tourist- Manama Bahrain by Mariel Diaz offers the inside scoop on Manama. Most travel books tell you how to travel like a tourist. Although there is nothing wrong with that, as part of the Greater Than a Tourist series, this book will give you travel tips from someone who has lived at your next travel destination.

In these pages, you will discover advice that will help you throughout your stay. This book will not tell you exact addresses or store hours but instead will give you excitement and knowledge from a local that you may not find in other smaller print travel books.

Travel like a local. Slow down, stay in one place, and get to know the people and the culture. By the time you finish this book, you will be eager and prepared to travel to your next destination.

TABLE OF CONTENTS

DEDICATION

This book is dedicated to my family and friends and to my Bahraini family. Thank you for giving me, teaching me, and showing me so much.

Bahrain, its culture and its people have definitely made me a reacher.

ABOUT THE AUTHOR

Mariel is a flight attendant and writer who lives in Bahrain. Having moved into the kingdom in 2015 to start a new chapter in her aviation career, Mariel calls Bahrain home. The weather and her love for water sports were the two key elements that brought her to the island. Soon she realised that Bahrain has much more to offer.

 She spends her time in the water, paddle-boarding or kitesurfing, and enjoying the beach days with her pug named Freddie Banana.

She enjoys live music and exploring the island in general, always discovering new places.

After completing a Tourism diploma she wanted to travel the world and decided to become a flight attendant. This profession has taken her around the world and has given her the chance to live in London Paris, Brussels and Tokyo.

Writing is her big love and after moving to Bahrain she completed a travel writing course and focused on writing poetry.

HOW TO USE THIS BOOK

The Greater Than a Tourist book series was written by someone who has lived in an area for over three months. The goal of this book is to help travelers either dream or experience different locations by providing opinions from a local. The author has made suggestions based on their own experiences. Please do your own research before traveling to the area in case the suggested places are unavailable.

FROM THE PUBLISHER

Traveling can be one of the most important parts of a person's life. The anticipation and memories that you have are some of the best. As a publisher of the Greater Than a Tourist book series, as well as the popular 50 Things to Know book series, we strive to help you learn about new places, spark your imagination, and inspire you. Wherever you are and whatever you do I wish you safe, fun, and inspiring travel.

Lisa Rusczyk Ed. D.
CZYK Publishing

OUR STORY

Traveling is a passion of the "Greater than a Tourist" series creator. Lisa studied abroad in college, and for their honeymoon Lisa and her husband toured Europe. During her travels to Malta, an older man tried to give her some advice based on his own experience living on the island since he was a young boy. She was not sure if she should talk to the stranger but was interested in his advice. When traveling to some places she was wary to talk to locals because she was afraid that they weren't being genuine. Through her travels, Lisa learned how much locals had to share with tourists. Lisa created the "Greater Than a Tourist" book series to help connect people with locals. A topic that locals are very passionate about sharing.

9

WELCOME TO
> TOURIST

INTRODUCTION

*The best things in life are the
people we love, the places we´ve
seen and the memories we´ve made
along the way.*

-Unknown.

a

1.GETTING OF THE PLANE

Once you have landed at Bahrain international airport you will have to get a visitor visa.

Find information online or at your embassy about visas, getting around, cultural events happening etc.

Bahrain International airport is quite small but another terminal is currently under construction and will be finished by 2019.

Make sure you are well informed prior your arrival about the items you are allowed to bring into the country. Should you want to purchase alcohol in the duty-free, I recommend you to double check with customs as the allowance permitted into the country changes quite often.

Currently, you are allowed to bring cigarettes not exceeding (400) cigarettes in quantity, (50) Cigars, (250) Grams of tobacco in open packets. Alcoholic Liquor is allowed into Bahrain if it does not exceed 1 liter and 6 cans of beer, only for non-Muslim passengers.

Also if you are planning to stay in the country for a while you might consider getting a sim card. The mobile operator Batelco has a stand at the duty-free shop where you can get a prepaid sim card. There are other mobile operators on the island like Viva. Viva has a shop at the terminal in arrivals. You will be able to get a sim card outside the airport at any of the main mobile operators, Batelco, Viva and Zain.

Wifi is available at the airport and in a wide range of cafes, restaurants and shopping malls.

Of course, make sure to switch your roaming off to prevent extra charges.

2.CURRENCY

The currency used in Bahrain is the Bahraini Dinar or BD. This currency is pegged to the US dollar which means the exchange rate would be the same whatever happens on the markets. You can exchange your currency directly at the airport at arrivals.

Another option will be to whit draw cash straight from an ATM machine, also available at the arrivals terminal.

There are plenty of exchange facilities in shopping malls and supermarkets round the island.

3.WINTER FUN

Winter in Bahrain runs from November to March and it can be pretty cold with average temperatures between 50 and 68 °F . Taking into consideration that temperatures in the summer months (from April to October) are average 104 °F and can reach 118.4 °F during June and July; we do get to wear boots and jackets and sip hot chocolate.

I arrived in the island in May 2015 and I got a slap of humidity and heat as soon as I step out of the plane. Did I bring any winter clothes with me ? No I didn´t.

As soon as November arrived with its rainy and windy days I realised I had totally underestimated the winter in the dessert.

Sky is beautifully clear blue in Bahrain in the winter and sunsets are stunning. I will take you to my favourite spots to watch the sunsets in detail later on.

Don't let the cooler weather discourage you. Activities like go karting, camping in the dessert, horse riding, cycling, golfing or even just taking a walk are very pleasant in the cooler months.

Wind blows in Bahrain during the winter months. We get visitors from neighbour countries willing to enjoy the windy conditions and practise windsurf and kitesurf. The water can be chilly so I recommend you bring a wetsuit and something warm to wear after the water.

4.GETTING AROUND

The easiest way to get around in the little island would be to rent a car. Driving can be quite challenging, specially on the weekends. It is easy to get around using a navigation like Google Maps or Waze.

Taxis are a most expensive option. Uber is also available in the Island , so it is Careem and Bahrain taxi online. You just need to download the app. Make sure the drivers understand where are you heading to.

Uber gets you anywhere. I remember on my first weeks in the island I decided to go kitesurfing in a remote lagoon and I took an Uber. The car got stuck in the sand while dropping me in the middle of nowhere. It was 113 degrees outside and it took us a while to get the car going again. Even so he came to pick me up once I´ve finished . Bahraini citizens are vey helpful and friendly.

If you are unlucky and get a flat tyre, this has happen to me a few times unfortunately, people is always willing to help you change it. I remember once I called a friend to help me changing a tyre and two people stop by and offer me help during the twenty minutes my friend took to arrive.

If you decide to drive, we drive on the right side of the road. There are speed cameras on the roads and some more are been installed. You might encounter police checks spread around the island, often at night time.

A little piece of advice I would give to visitors driving in the country is check your right mirror constantly as other drivers tend to overtake from the right, usually at high speed.

It is against the law to drink and drive in Bahrain. The alcohol permitted in the blood stream is 0.0%. The advice really needs to be – not to drink at all when driving.

You will have to pay by cash when refuelling so bear that in mind.

Traffic can be very hectic in the island, specially on weekends and bank holidays. We receive visitors from Saudi Arabia as they just have to cross a bridge to get here. There is a high chance of getting stuck in a traffic jam in and out Manama, so plan your journey ahead.

5.PASHMINA AND LIGHT JACKET, A MUST.

Ladies will be required to dress conservatively in some places like shopping malls, mosques, souks, government facilities etc.This is cover your knees and shoulders. Also you don´t want to attract too much attention. I recommend always carry a pashmina or light jacket with you, it will be a light saver as It will allow you everywhere.

One of the few "troubles" we ladies encounter here in the Middle East is the dress code.

With time I learnt, long trousers or maxi dresses will take you everywhere. Shorts and tank tops just for the beach or pool. A cardigan can save you a trip back to your hotel to change.

Also air conditionings are very strong in some buildings so you are better safe than sorry.

6.BAHRAIN TOUR GUIDES

If you are willing to explore but you would rather do it assisted by a tour guide, Bahrain Tour guides is your best bet. Check them out on instagram on "bahraintourguides" where they post stunning pictures of what you can find in the Kingdom.

They have local guides Licensed by Tourism Authority, often multilingual. They offer half a day tours and also tailor made experiences if there is something that you specifically like to do like horse riding, a fishing trip or pearl diving .

I tried them myself and I absolute recommend their trips. You will get to experience the "real" Bahrain.

I took a tour called "Walk of life" where I got to discover the old city of Muharraq, ancient capital of the Kingdom. Walking around these old streets filled with history, turning the corner to white narrow little passages, Greek alike, visiting the cultural homes beautifully preserved, letting your creative side meet your mind in the hidden art galleries and research centres and ending up with a coffee or a fresh juice in an unique emplacement is a great way of discovering Bahraini culture and heritage.

Their tour guides are very approachable and professional and wiling to answer any question you might have.

What is your favourite place in the whole Bahrain? Was my question to my tour guide, Bader.

I love all Bahrain. I cant decide on one only place he said smiling broadly. I could tell that he really has a passion for his job, his country and wants to transmit it to visitors.

7.FANCY GRABBING BREAKFAST?

Food in general is a very big part of Bahraini culture. Breakfast is a very popular social activity among expats and locals. There are numerous cafes spread around the island and the variety goes from traditional Bahraini breakfast, continental, organic, vegan to full english breakfast.

For an authentic local experience head to Emmawash in Budaiya.

Emmawsh is a very charming traditional restaurant located in a busy road full of little shops and cafes. It might not tell you anything from the outside as all you will see is a little terrace with very basic wooden furniture. Once you get inside the game changes. On the ground floor you will find wooden benches and tables covered with typical Bahraini table clothes. The charm of this place is that the white walls are covered in draws, quotes, words. People goes to Emmawash not only to socialise and enjoy a very tasty traditional affordable breakfast. People goes to this place to make statements on the walls and to read what people have to say. Don´t be shy and request a marker so you can leave your statement to the world on walls and ceilings.

On the top floor they also serve breakfast, while you are sat on the floor, a very unique experience.

Being a writer myself I enjoy going to Emmawash and leave some of my favourite quotes and words impregnated in the place. When I visit again I love to spend time trying to find my words and remember why did I wrote them.Theres so much personal experiences and stories in this building!

Another well known venue for breakfast is Saffron by Jenna in Shaikh Salman Fort, also called Riffa Fort.

Doors carved with Qur'anic verses will welcome you to this charismatic emplacement.

They offer a Bahraini breakfast set so you can try a bit of everything.

The best part of this venue is the terrace overlooking the valley. Breakfast is served here in the cooler months. Make sure you double check with them that their are opened before taking the thirty minutes drive from Manama.

You can find another branch of Saffron by Jenna beautifully located in Muharraq Souk.

Hard to decide what to order? Here is a list of the most common items of Arabic breakfast that will make the job easy.

Balaleet: Sweet vermicelli topped with an omelet.

Baydh Tomat: Eggs scrambled with crushed fresh tomatoes.

Nikhee: Chickpeas fried in a Bahraini-style sauce.

Alo Chab: Fried potato kababs.

Alo: Sautéed potatoes with Bahraini spices.

Khubz Tannoor: Traditional Bahraini flat bread with fish sauce.

Karak: Tea brewed in evaporated milk.

Chai Haleeb (Tea with Milk): Tea brewed in fresh milk flavoured with cardamom.

Nomad Eatery is a most contemporary option. It is located in a small mall called The Courtyard, in Seef area. The deco is chic, modern, urban and very cozy. Have a look at the display of lamps, chandeliers and bulbs hanging from the ceiling, they leave me staring in amusement every time I go to Nomad.

If you are a coffee lover this place will feel like heaven. The wide selection of coffees is to die for.

I invite you to try the nitro coffee. It is a cold tasty brewed coffee, one of the most popular coffees on the menu. It can be served black or with milk. Their hazelnut milk and almond milk options are another reason to try this place.

They use three different ways of brewing coffees and serve award winning speciality coffees like Taf. Taf comes from Greece and its committed to sustainability.

Lets talk food. This eatery offers breakfast lunch and dinner. The menu is impressive. Choices go as far as açai bowls, eggs, pizzas, pasta, poke bowls.

A visit to this award wining eatery is not to be missed.

8.NATIONAL MUSEUM

Located half way in Between Manama and Muharraq you will notice this impressive building right in front of the water. Its nine halls will take you on a journey of Bahraini culture and heritage offering you a visual glimpse of the life in the Kingdom through handcrafts, documents and manuscripts.

Several international culture and art exhibitions are often hosted at Bahrain National Museum. Check their website for updated information:

End your visit with a boat tour across the bay to Muharraq to have a very memorable experience.

9.LET'S GET CRAFTY

If you would like to indulge in art activities while meeting expats and locals and socialise pay a visit to Masq Art space in Budaiya. There is so much art going on in between this four bohemian walls! They provide drawing lessons, Arabic calligraphy classes, painting courses, photography and fashion design courses. They also host stand up comedies, movie screenings, concerts and exhibitions. Even if you do not wish to take any classes or participate in any activity the visit is worthy. Take a look at someone else's creation in this welcoming community. Sit down and enjoy a fresh juice while chatting with the friendly staff about whats happening in the island.

10.BEST SUNSETS

One of the best sunsets in Bahrain can be spotted from Sofitel Zallaq Thalassa sea & spa hotel situated in the west coast of the Island. The sun meets the sea while paints delicately brushed orange tonalities. You can simply sit down at their private beach and enjoy the sun saying its goodnights into the pristine waters. Sofitel also offers a picnic set up the beach. This will be undoubtedly a very special memory of your trip to Bahrain!

Witness a very stunning sunset also from Amwaj Island. Kitebeach in Amwaj is one of my favourites sunset spots and I try no to miss it. If you are travelling on a budget or you rather prepare your own sunset picnic, go grocery shopping at Alosra supermarket, Amwaj branch. Prepare a blanket or a beach towel, chill out tunes, refreshments and voila, perfect sunset and perfect memory to take back home. The beauty of the sunsets in Amwaj apart from the twilight itself is that you can catch sight of a mosque in the other side of the bay, right where the sun is setting. This is a perfect spot for a picture.

Wuu lounge in Art Rotana hotel is another place where I like to go watch the sun disappear in the sea while listening to the djs latest beats and sipping sundowners.

Clears skies and the variety of exotic colours are a delight for sunset lovers while visiting the tiny Island.

11.TRAVELLING WITH KIDS

The variety of activities for the little ones in Bahrain is extensive. When is too hot outside to even

walk, visit the indoor water park Wahooo ,at City
Center Shopping mall. This is the first indoor
waterpark in the Middle East. The exciting rides,
slides and attractions are suitable for all ages. There is
a toddler pool and a wave pool.

Magic Island is an indoor theme park located in
Seef Mall. It has six themed zones with attractions for
kids all ages. There are bumper cars, rides, simulator
games, bowling, minigolf etc.

There are trampoline parks like Jump up in Ramli
Mall, Isa Town. They host "Toddler day time" events
and the accept online bookings. Trampolines are also
for adults for all of you with a kid inside like me.

Explore your kids creative side with a visit to
Studio Ceramics in Seef Mall, or Artzania, Ramli
Mall. These studios offer clay building, painting,
crafts ceramic painting for children. The kids can
either join a lesson or express freely their artistic side.

Pamper the little ones at Lalapaloza junior spa in
Al A`li Shopping Complex or Hello Kitty Beauty Spa
in City Center. They have spa treatments and

pampering sessions specially designed for the little ones.

As you can see options are wide when it comes to kids entertainment. Some outdoors activities that the whole family can enjoy together are horse riding, visit camel farms, a day at the beach, go karting, adventure park etc.

12. MUSIC FESTIVALS

Trib Fest happens twice a year, once in autumn an once in spring at Rugby Club. Its an open air family friendly festival featuring more than 20 tribute acts. Trib Fest is a great occasion to spend the day with family and friends, do a picnic in the grass and enjoy the live music. The line up is announced in advance on their website. The event is one of the favourites on Bahrain social calendar. It runs from 10 am to 10 pm and food and drinks are available at the venue. For those who still feel like dancing the night away, Rugby club remains opened once the life music is over, offering very affordable food and drinks.

Another well known music festival is the Jazz Fest that takes place at the Royal Golf Club. Usually celebrated in the month of October, it is a family-friendly music event featuring iconic performances by award winning international and local artists.

In the venue there are day markets, trendy food trucks and a kids area.

Mingle with locals and expats and enjoy a fun day out. This is one of my favourite festivals. Plan your visit ahead if you are driving to make sure you don't struggle with finding a parking spot. Carpool is always a very good option.

13. FRIDAY BRUNCH

Probably the most common way of celebrating birthday parties, family and work events among the residents. Pay a fee and enjoy unlimited food and drinks usually from 12 to 4pm.

There are countless brunches happening on Friday for all tastes and budgets.

Crown Plaza brunch is well known among the younger crowd. They have a life band and entertainment. They offer discount to military personnel.

Four Seasons, Sofitel, Movenpick and Rotana hotels host big Friday brunches with a wide variety of food stations and beverages, alcoholic and non alcoholic. They provide life entertainment and they are very popular brunch choices.

If you are looking for something cosier and less overwhelming try The Foundry brunch. Their menu is outstanding, their atmosphere is chic and cosy and their cocktails just delightful.

A less expensive option will be Wembleys, also well known by the expats crowd. Their food selection is basic but tasty. Their setting simulating an outdoors beer garden and their life entertainment are just fun. If you are feeling adventurous feel free to go and perform at the stage .

14. PAMPERING

Craving a nice massage? Or maybe a pedicure or manicure? What about a Moroccan bath?

Argan spa in Amwaj offers a ladies and a gents spa separately. On their menu you will find all kind of beauty treatments and they usually have package promotions. Their services and facilities are impeccable.

Four Seasons is another place not to miss when looking for a bit of pampering. The spa ambience is inviting and very relaxing. You will get transported to a real Arabic spa experience. On the menu you can find very high quality beauty treatments from facias, slimming treatments, massages etc. Their signature Bahrain massages will rejuvenate your body and mind.

There are beauty salons for all budgets and treatments across Bahrain. If you just need a manicure or pedicure or a quick blow dry before heading out for dinner, Bahrain has very competitive prices, usually cheaper than Europe.

15. ADLIYA

Adliya is a renowned area of restaurants, cafes and art galleries located in the centre of Manama.

Take a walk in this charming neighbourhood with pedestrian streets filled up with local art.

This chic district is also home to townhouses turned into art galleries, like Gallery21.

One of my favourite places for an afternoon coffee and a cake is Al Riwaq art cafe. I love to sit outside and just watch people passing by or read a good book. I usually take a little wonder inside where the display of modern art in the walls keeps me entertained for hours.

There is a huge selection of restaurants and cafes in the streets of Adlyia. International restaurants like meat.co , Spanish cuisine like Vinoteca Barcelona, greek cuisine like Attik, local cuisine like Cocos, Asian like Meisei.

When the weather is nice the rooftops of this multicultural area get packed with people enjoying dinner or drinks and socialising.

Adliya is a big part of the Bahraini nightlife. At the entrance of the main pedestrian street you can find a big "I love Bahrain" sign, the perfect location for graphic memory of your visit to the country.

16. AL FATEH GRAND MOSQUE

The Grand Mosque is situated next to the King Faisal Highway in Juffair. it is one of the biggest touristic attractions in Bahrain. Its opened for visit every day except Fridays. The entrance to the Mosque is free and you will get a guide. You will have to dress conservatively for your visit, however an abaya (traditional muslim loose over garment) will be provided for your visit.

17. THE SOUKS

For a taste of ancient Arabic culture head to the souks. Its narrow streets full of little old shops selling everything from garments, homeware, spices , animals; will offer you a different perspective of the old traditional Bahrain. You can often smell rose water or cardamon while wondering around. Its hectic traffic, busy streets, cars honking and prayers coming from the nearby mosques will transfer you to the trading era.

Goods like cotton and wood are better purchased here. Spices and herbs like cardamon, cinnamon, cumin, curry are sold everywhere in the Souks.

Muharraq souk is the best place to purchase the Bahraini traditional sweet, Halwa.

There are also plenty of tailor little shops available. I recommend you to purchase a tailor made suit or dress if you have time. They are affordable in the Souks.

18. GOLF

The Royal Golf club is located in Riffa. About 30 min driving from Manama.

It is the only 18 hole championship standard golf course and a par 3 9-hole course.

Additional facilities at the Royal Golf Club include award winning restaurants, a golf academy with full practice facilities, a golf & leisure shop, meeting and conference rooms and a country club.

19. SAFETY

Have you ever forgotten your mobile phone in a taxi and got it back the same day with no problems? I have, several times. This is how safe Bahrain is. Residents are warm and friendly welcoming visitors. If you loose something it gets returned in most of the cases. We don't have to worry about locking the car doors, placing handbags on chairs when sat outside or items on tables. Robberies and pick pocketing in the Kingdom are very very rare.

20. THE HOLY MONTH OF RAMADAN

The beginning and end of Ramadan are determined by the lunar Islamic calendar so its changes every year and it is announced very last minute.

Ramadan is celebrated every year in the Arabic countries. It is time to practice self-restraint; a time to cleanse the body and soul from impurities and re-focus one's self on the worship of God.

If you happen to visit Bahrain during Ramadan this is a good time to get involved with local traditions. Many hotels and restaurants host nightly Iftar banquets, no better occasion than this to try the local dishes.

Iftar is the name given to the evening meal when Muslims break their fast during the Islamic month of Ramadan. Iftar is one of the religious observances of Ramadan and is often done as a community. Families usually break their fast together after sunset. A date will be the first thing consumed when breaking the fast.

Some things to take into consideration when visiting Bahrain during Ramadan are:

Drink, eat, smoke and chew chewing gum in the privacy of your home or hotel room from sunrise to sunset.

Office hours will change adapting to fasting and praying hours. Double check with the establishment you wish to visit beforehand.

Avoid driving close to sunset. Roads will be packed and drivers rushing to break their fast.

Dress conservatively, covering shoulders, knees and necklines.

Alcoholic beverages are not served in any establishment during the holy month and music won't be played.

This does not mean you can not visit Bahrain during Ramadan, visitors are more than welcome. However having to adapt to the fasting rules, ramadan special schedules, hectic traffic right before Iftar might be challenging.

The first year I moved to Bahrain my birthday fall into Ramadan. I celebrated it with an Iftar dinner at Gulf Hotel in a traditional Iftar tent . I loved every second of it.

21. FUN IN THE SUN

Options are very large when it comes to have a beach day. There are beaches where you can practise water sports, some family oriented, private beaches, public access ones etc.

Tala Beach: Tala belongs to the Amwaj Islands. It is a private residential area with villas and short cute buildings. Their beach is for public access. To enter the beach just head in between some of the buildings right before the security gate at Tala. I would call it more a lagoon. There is a strip of sand around this beach / lagoon for those wishing to lounge and sunbathe . You can bring your own bbq, floaty, chairs etc. In the weekends there are a lots of families. The beach offers no facilities so be aware. It a good beach for paddle boarding due to their flat water. The perfect place to relax in the sun low key.

Kite Beach: Another public beach located in Amwaj Island. The kitesurfer community gave the name to this beach as is the place they use to practise kitesurf and windsurf. Kitebeach offers stunning sunsets with straight view to Marassi beach and the mosque. There are no facilities in this beach and the sea can be quite rocky.

Marassi Beach: Possibly one of the newest beaches in Bahrain. Marassi opened to the public in is a private beach and you will have to pay a reasonable fee to use this beach. The beach is stunning, fine sand, clean water, facilities as toilets, showers. There is a little water sports centre offering parasailing and a little cable park.

If you don't want to carry your own food an drinks with you, there are food trucks available and a cafe.

My piece of advice would be check with them beforehand If ladies are allowed in bikini in Marassi as the rule has changed numerous times.

Marina Beach Amwaj: Situated also in Amwaj , at the Marina, is the place to morn boats and yachts. The Marina also has a little beach. It gets quite busy in the weekends and the amount of noisy jetsskys driving around might look similar than a highway. The beach has facilities like toilets and sun beds.

Private beaches: Most of the big hotels in the Kingdom have a private beach with facilities and food and drinks service. You can access those fabulous beaches for free if you are staying in their hotel, or purchase a daily pass.

Hotels with a private beach in Bahrain are the Art Rotana in Amwaj, Ritz Carlton, Fours seasons, Royal Sarai Jumeirah and Sofitel.

Needles to say that you have all the facilities and the beaches are very clean and taken care of.

If you are not a fan of salty water and you rather chill poolside thats also possible. Hotels like Rotana, Intercontinental or beach bars Like Coral Bay have pools that can be accessed paying a fee.

Beach and pool parties: regardless of you been a beach lover or a pool lover, as soon as you are a music lover there is a party for you. The major hotels with private beach and pool organise beach/ pool parties. The crowd differ from place to place and depends of the music style and theme of the party.

Coral bay organises electronic music parties and also reggae nights.

Intercontinental Hotel hosts big pool side day parties.

Rotana Amwaj host pool day parties. You will require to pay an entry fee in most of them.

Jumeriah hotel opened his doors recently and organised a few pop up parties.

The Ritz Carlton hotel hosts exclusive night beach parties. Their white party is one of the most popular. They have an attractive buffet right on the beach, unlimited drinks and live entertainment with a stage situated right on the sand. Ladies, leave your high heels at home. Do purchase your tickets in advance for this parties as they get sold out quick.

22. WHATS HAPPENING WHERE

With multiple activities happening at the same time all over Bahrain I recommend you to check the events agenda so you can plan your schedule and events you will like to attend.

Choices are for all tastes when it comes to events . Marathons and other sport events, music events like jazz nights or concerts, exhibitions etc. Check Time out Bahrain (printed or online edition) , Bahrain this month, Radio Bahrain on the 96,5 dial and calendar.bh for the latest updates of whats is happening and where.

23. SMOKERS

Most of the restaurants and cafes in Bahrain have a designated smoking area but it is not the case when it comes to clubs and lounge bars. In most of the clubs and pubs guest are allowed to smoke inside in the common areas. I often bring eye drops with me to prevent my eyes to get irritated when at smoky places.

Shisha is an important part of socialising for Bahrainis. You can find shisha bars literally everywhere.

24. WHERE TO STAY

The first question I would ask you is , would you like to enjoy the sea in a quiet environment? Would you like to enjoy the City? Would you like to have both city and sea?

If you prefer a quiet place to stay, close to the sea, and then take trips to the city to enjoy what it has to offer, then Amwaj is ideal.

Amwaj Island is an artificial island and residential neighbourhood only ten minutes drive from the airport. There is a big community of expats living in Amwaj and a few hotels accommodation wise. The advantage of staying here is that you can enjoy peaceful and quiet beaches and walks outdoors. But for most of cultural sights and activities you will have to travel to Manama. The drive to Manama takes approximately twenty minutes, always depending of the traffic conditions.

A recommendable option to stay in Amwaj would be the Art Rotana Hotel and Resort

It is located right in front of a private beach and it features a swimming pool, spa, eight international restaurants and a fitness centre.

If you prefer to remainIn the city centre and at close distance of most of Shopping malls, nightlife but also in front of the sea Royal Jumeirah Sarai, Ritz Carlton, Four season are great choices.

For those that like the comfort of an apartment with facilities, check air b and b.

25.GENTS LEAVE YOUR FLIP FLOPS AND SHORTS FOR THE SEA OR POOL

In most of the restaurants you will be denied the entrance if you show up in shorts or flip flops. This rule is strictly followed. Long trousers and shoes will guaranty you the access to dining and soirees places.

26. STAY FIT, TRY NEW THINGS

The variety of indoor gyms and fitness centres in Bahrain is very large. You will be able to try a free class of pole dancing, spinning, aeroyoga, dance etc in most of the fitness centres. Day passes are available for purchase in most of the gyms.

Willing to try new things? Download the app Guavapass. This app gives you a monthly unlimited membership allowing you to book and enjoy fitness classes across Asia. You can also purchase four classes in four different studios to enjoy during your stay in the Kingdom.

Some of the classes you can book in Guavapass are: Muai thai, yoga, dance, pilates, open gym, spinning, zumba, meditation, boot camp, aeroyoga, pool, boxing, aqua aerobics, trx, body pump, butt and abs, spartacus weights, circuit training, piloxing, hiit and much more.

27. STAY HYDRATED

No matter where you go, always bring water with you. The heat, dust and humidity will dehydrate your body before you notice it. Drinking tap water is not recommendable. If you would like to give your body a little bit extra purchase minerals to add to your water. You can find those in any pharmacy. They will help you feel revitalised and with more energy.

28. LADIES NIGHTS

There is such a thing in the Middle East as "Ladies Nights" where we get unlimited, or in some cases limited complimentary drinks in bars, clubs and pubs. Yes, we are lucky, indeed.

Ladies nights are hosted in different venues and at different days of the week.

One of the best Ladies Nights is in Gallery 21 (Adliya) on Wednesdays from 9 pm to 11pm.

You can sip high quality cocktails in their trendy rooftop while dancing the night away to the latest cool beats.

Monday night means Chic Mondays in Play Restaurant and Lounge. This indoor venue is situated in Jumeirah Royal Saray Hotel. Expect three complimentary cocktails for ladies from 9 pm until 2 am. Dance to R&B beats in a stylish and elegant atmosphere.

For the latin music lovers try Players Lounge every Wednesday from 8pm to 12am. Chica Bonita Nights are nights filled with salsa, bachata and kizomba moves.

Check straight away with the venues to get up to date information about laddies nights.

29. SPRING OF CULTURE

The Kingdom is on fire during the month of March. Not only the weather is amazing making possible to enjoy any kind of day or night activities, indoors and outdoors. The Spring of Culture is celebrated in the Kingdom every year in March ad they are currently on their 14th edition.

This fun filled month brings together artists, musicians, exhibitions and art in all form and shapes from all over the world.

The events calendar is published on their website and main Bahraini magazines and newspapers.

Countless exhibitions, lectures, concerts and shows set the Island in a festive vibe. There is something happening in nearly every museum, art gallery, fort and concert hall.

I always try to attend as many events as possible going to exhibitions during the day and staying downtown to enjoy concerts at night.

Tip, If you travel downtown for two or more events, stay in town for the next one because driving in and out Manama and searching for parking spot can take hours.

30. NOT YOUR USUAL SPA EXPERIENCE

La Fontaine not only is an historical building, its also home to a spa, a contemporary art centre and a fine dining experience.

Located in the hearth of Manama, the Kingdoms capital, in between busy narrow streets and dirty old buildings you will find this hidden gem.

The property which belongs to the Alizera family reminds of an ancient European chateau.

The spa is located at the top floor offering beautiful views of Manama. They offer all kind of beauty treatments and also a package deal should you be travelling in a group.

Take a walk inside the inviting art rooms where you can find different exhibitions by local and foreign artists. Go shopping in the cozy jewellery shop featuring exquisite pieces designed by local artist.

Fancy a cocktail or maybe dinner? La Fontaine offers you a fine dinning experience in its beautiful restaurant or patio should the weather be inviting. Old jazz tunes in the background, exquisite deco, carefully selected plants and a fountain presiding the patio are just the perfect setting to a romantic dinner.

31. DAY TRIP TO NEARBY ISLANDS

Take a bot trip to Jarada island and get to swim in crystal clear waters and sunbathe in the sandbank. The beautiful strip of white sand disappears with the high tide. You can spot manta rays and dolphins on the way.

Take a boat from Sitra Fishermans port to Al Dar Beach resort. This natural beach its only 8 minutes away offshore. Chalets and beach huts are available for rent. There are also facilities at Al Dar like bar, sun beds, volleyball court and water sport rentals.

Check them out online and find out about fees, timings and activities.

32. PEARL DIVING

Pearl fishing has been happening in Bahrain since 3000 years. Visitors have the chance to take a pearl diving tour where they can pick their own oysters hoping there is a pearl inside. You can purchase your tickets online or with Bahrain Tour Guides. You will depart from Ras Rayyah with a licensed diving and collect up to 60 oysters in this unique diving experience. Pearls found will be appraised for value and quality.

Bahrain Tour guides offers customised pearl diving trips.

If you prefer buy your own pearls head to Manama souk. There are multiple jewellery stores at the souk where authentic Bahraini pearls are available for purchase.

33. SOUVENIRS AND THINGS TO BUY

Dates: Bahrain is famous for its dates. Dates are normally served with Arabic coffee when welcoming guest. You can also add them to a smoothie as a source of fibre and antioxidants.

Purchase gourmet dates at Bateel stored located in City Center Mall.

Pearls: Bahrain is one of the best places to purchase pearls. You will be able to find pearls and pieces jewellery made of pearls at Manama Souk.

Necklace with your name written in Arabic, also available in the souk.

Pottery: available in many stores. A´ali and Delmon pottery are two well known stores.

Tailor made suits and dresses: Everywhere at the Souks.

34. THE FORTS

Bahrain forts are few of the historical gems of the Kingdom.

Bahrain Fort or Qal'at Al Bahrain became Bahrain's first Unesco World Heritage Site in 2005. It has been turned into a museum and its the place where I always bring friends and family.

What makes it so special? It is in front of the sea, very well preserved and there are walking paths surrounding this impressive piece of history. It is an idilic place to take a walk or enjoy an afternoon coffee while soaking up the sun and stunning views. If you are a photography lover, do not forget your camera at home. You will get incredible shots at sunset.

Drive across the Island to visit Riffa fort. This fort is smaller than Bahrains fort and unlike the first one, it is not by the sea. Building is very well preserved and it offers visitors a glimpse of life back in 1982.

One of the branches of Saffron by Jena restaurant is located at Riffa Fort. I recommend you to sit outside in the delightful terrace and enjoy a drink or a meal while overlooking the Hunanaiya valley.

Lastly have a look at Arad fort, built in the 15th century. It is magic when the sun starts to go down. This fort is used as an outdoor musical venue.

35. A CLEAN ISLAND IS A HAPPY ISLAND

Residents of Bahrain are becoming more and more aware of the importance of no littering and keeping the shores clean, however, there is still a lot of work to do.

Unfortunately you will encounter bags, plastic bottles and all kind of objects when you take a stroll at Bahrain public beaches. By no littering you are already contributing. If you would like to go an extra mile take a bag with you and collect the waste lying on the shores.

Bahrain beach combers is an organisation trying to bring awareness into Bahrain inhabitants. They organise periodical beach cleaning days in the different public shores of the island. Search them of facebook for more information and feel free to join when visiting the country.

36. PDA

Public displays of affection are generally not tolerated in Bahrain. It might be difficult to keep this in mind when you come from a different culture. Try to adhere to the rule and be sensible and respectful. Public display is considered inappropriate and even offensive to some.

37. FORMULA ONE

The Bahrain International Circuit located in Sakhir desert hosts the yearly Formula One Grand Prix. This is an event not to miss for all motorsport enthusiasts. Check out their website to find out about formula one and other events taking place in this venue such a marathons, concerts etc.

bahraingp.com

38. LOCAL DISHES TO TRY

Machboos: A dish made with mutton, chicken, or fish accompanied over fragrant rice that has been cooked in chicken/mutton well spiced broth. My favourite is fish machboos. One of the perks of live in an island is the delicious fresh fish.

Biriany is a very common dish, which consists of heavily seasoned rice cooked with chicken or lamb. Originally from the Indian sub-continent.

Hummus: a dip consisting of mashed chickpeas (garbanzo beans), tahini, garlic, and lemon. There are plenty of variants when it come sto hummus. The chickpeas is the traditional recipe, but you can find avocado or beetroot hummus these days too. Delicious.

Falafel: fried chickpeas (garbanzo beans) balls served with vegetables in bread.

Shawarma, lamb or chicken carved from a rotating spit and wrapped in pita bread.

39. CARE FOR DESSERT?

For those with a sweet tooth you will be able to find all kind of sweets and desserts satisfying the most exquisite palates. From the usual cakes, carrot, chocolate fondant, eclairs, red velvet, cheese cakes to the local specialities.

Let me introduce you to the local specialities:

Baklava sweet pastry is made using layers of filo pastry, which are filled with chopped nuts (typically pistachios or walnuts) and held together with sticky honey or a syrup flavoured with rose water or orange blossom. It's then served at room temperature, and garnished with sprinklings of ground nuts.

Halwa

Is the most popular sweet of Bahrain. Its made from corn flour and there are a few varieties to choose from – red, green and golden, to name some. The most popular red version is mixed up with nuts (pistachios, almonds, walnuts), spices (cardamom, cinnamon, nutmeg, saffron) and rose water, plus plenty of sugar, to create a seriously flavourful, jelly-like sweet treat.

There is a Halwa factory located at Muharraq souk. You can smell the sweet making process from far.

Kunafa

Its the Middle Eats version of a cheesecake. Basically a cheese similar to mozzarella rolled in pastry or shredded phyllo dough, and topped with sugar- or honey-syrup. There are numerous ways to create this dish, but each variety brings something unique, and utterly delicious, to the table.

The local chain Kanafawy offers numerous varieties of this dessert. The main store is in Manama, near Al Samady Coffee Shop.

Luqaymat

There are little fried dough balls. Also known as luqmat al-kadhi, or 'Zainab Fingers', they're crispy on the outside, soft and squidgy on the inside and drenched in honey or sugar syrup, which is sometimes flavoured with saffron or cardamom. They're then often rolled in toasted sesame seeds for extra crunch.

The best Luqaymat in Bahrain is found in Emma-Wash restaurant in Budaiya.

Umm Ali

Umm Ali is arguably the Middle East's most famous dessert. It consist of a bread pudding made of puff pastry, condensed milk, cream, nuts, sultanas and shredded coconut.

Head back to popular bakery Saadeddin for some of the island's best umm ali.

40. JELLY FISH

Unfortunately Jelly fish pays a visit to our sea yearly. Bahraini waters are warm and welcoming for these sea creatures. Unluckily I have been stung a few times. There a lot of remedies you can find online that cal help you reduce the pain produced by jelly fish stung.

To me the most effective is vinegar and I always carry a bottle in my bag when I go boating.

Sweet water will only make it sting more and get more irritated. Scratching or rubbing the affected are a is a no no.

If you suspect you might be experiencing an allergic reaction when stung by a jelly fish visit a nearby hospital.

41. WATER SPORTS

What else would you do if you live in a territory surrounded by water? They say every day in the water is a good day. The numerous water sports activities you can do in the Kingdom fit every taste and fitness level.

Kitesurf.

One of the reasons I decided to move to Bahrain is life by the sea and Kitesurf. We have a friendly chilled out kitesurf community in the Island. The windiest months run from November to July.

In the summer we get a few windy days as well, if we are lucky. Kitesurfing in the summer in Bahrain can be a bit challenging because of the extremely hot temperatures but also fun to cruise around and soak in very warm water. Dont forget your flip flops or shoes when you hit the beach in the summer months. Ive learnt this to well after burning badly my soles.

There are two main kitesurf spots in the island. Kitebeach in Amwaj Island and Nurana lagoon.

The water is mainly flat. Kitesurf spots get a little bit more crowded during the weekends and bank holidays but are still enjoyable.

You can take lessons with the local schools Bliss Marine and Beach culture. Lessons are a must to learn this sport as there are many safety tips you will need to be aware of as well as wind directions, tides etc.

If you are a beginner do not worry. Head to the beach and the friendly kite instructors and fellow kitesurfers will keep an eye on you and offer you a hand when need it.

Windsurf.

There is also a windsurf community usually practising at Kitebeach. Lessons are also available at Beach culture.

Paddle board. You can practise this sport in very different locations around the island. There is Beach Culture offering paddle boarding tours and paddle yoga. Paddle into the sunset on a no windy day while the water is flat at kitebeach. Sunset by the sea while paddle boarding is a soul filling experience. This is an incredible memory to take home.

Wake board and water ski are also available. There is a cable park at Marassi beach.

If you would like to learn wakeboard Biss Marine is your best option. They are based at Amwaj Marina.

They offer individual and group lessons and provide you with al the equipment. Instructors are very professional and passionate about the sport.

For more water sports activities, diving lessons, sailing lessons etc , contact Biss Marine Amwaj.

42. WHAT TO BRING

Bring sunscreen as the sun is very strong in the kingdom and you will burn without realising.

Sun glasses for the same reason.They will also protect your eyes from dust or sand in windier days. You know is is very hot outside when you step out with your sunglasses and they all steamy making impossible to see.

Pashmina or light jacket to access official buildings and malls.

Flip flops is you are planing to go to the beach as the sand can get so hot you will burn your soles.

Shoes for the water if you are planing to get into places with rocks like kitebeach.

Long trousers and closed shoes if you are planing to dine out.

An open mind and willingness to meet people and blend into the community.

43. SHOPPING

I lost count on how many shopping malls we have on the island but I will point out the main ones.

City Centre is one of the biggest and most popular shopping mall. You can find the main high street shops you will be able to find elsewhere. There are also electronics, homeware, bank, cinema and even a water park and a food court. International clothing brands, the most popular, are sold here. Been one of the most popular malls it can get overwhelmingly busy specially o the weekends or sales season.

Seef Mall. It is as well a very popular mall with international brands and high street stores. What I like from Seef Mall is that there are a few local buotiques you wont find in any other mall. Also the indoor theme park, Magic Islands makes it pretty unique.

The Avenues. Recently opened changed the concept of shopping in the island. High street fashion, Fine dinning restaurants a promenade and cinema guarantee you an enjoyable time when visiting this mall.

Al Ali mall. Probably my favourite shopping mall. Easy, accessible and not too big. High street shops aren't available here. Al Ali mall is all about local designers, international renown high fashion brands and small boutiques. You can find exclusive fashion pieces here. Prices go a bit on the upscale but you can find some bargains specially on sales. This mall is also home to some exclusive cafes and restaurants like The Florist's Daughter. A very special boutique restaurant, cafe and a beautiful flowershop.

Moda Mall. Hosting the most luxury brands and haute couture.

44. CAMEL FARMS

Visit the Bahrain Royal Camel farm for a great family day out. Visitors have the opportunity to get up close and personal with the camels, feeding and touching them. Located in Manama, just off the

Janabiyah highway, The Royal Camel Farm is open every day from 8am to 5pm and is free to enter.

45. EVERYTHING DELIVERED TO YOUOR DOOR STEEP

And I mean everything. You only have to phone the cold stores opened 24 hours. They are small supermarkets with supplies of a bit of everything. You run out of deodorant or shampoo? Need some ice? Maybe you need batteries for your camera? Craving a late night snack or chocolate? They will deliver it, no matter what your location is, without extra charge.

46. MARKETS

One of the things I always do when I travel to a different destination is to visit a local market. I might not look forward to buy anything in particular, but I get a glimpse of what life it is like.

The farmers market in Salmabad is one of my favourite ones. It opens everyday from 8 am until 3 pm. The selection of fresh fruits and vegetables in this market is huge. The prices are very affordable and the quality is excellent. Tourists, locals, merchants, they all mix in this market.

Another market growing in popularity is Budaiya farmers market. It only goes to October to April. In addition to the food stands there is a food court in case you fancy grabbing a bite here. It can get quite crowded and to find a parking spot might become a challenge. I recommend you visit the markets early in the morning to have the best experience.

47. NIGHLIFE

Nightlife is exciting, vibrant and busy in the Kingdom. It is concentrated in different districts and it can go from a quiet chilled lounge bar to a karaoke to a crazy electronic music festival.

Adlya is one of the most busy areas when talking about nightlife. There are countless bars and rooftops serving drinks and playing the latest beats.

If you are looking for a classy trendy place where you can enjoy a cocktail Hazel is a very good option. This indoors roof top has developed to be one of the "it" places in Bahrain. They host life music concerts a few nights per week. Cocktails selection, food and service are very fine.

You can sit down and enjoy a nice conversation without going wild. It is a very chic and trendy venue.

Lanters Gastro pub is the place to go after brunch. They have a restaurant, a bar area and a roof top. It usually gets very busy at happy our. There is a open patio with air conditioning at Lanters, one of my favourite traits of this place.

Olivetto is a stylish Italian restaurant and lounge bar. They host parties pool side in an elegant ambiance.

Jj´s is the place to go for karaoke, a casual night out and cheap beverages. Its and old Irish pub , dark and smoky, and a lot of fun. Their drinks are very affordable and the crowd is very laid back.

Calexico is a Mexican restaurant and cocktail bar. They have a dance floor ,high quality cocktails and a dj entertaining with the latest commercial hits. Try their ginger beer and of course their tequila shots.

The amount of lounge bars, roof top terraces and pubs in Adliya is countless. you just have to take a walk around during the weekend nights, Thursday and Friday in Bahrain, and ask the people where is the party happening.

Juffair is another district where the nightlife action happens. There are sport bars like Wembleys, pubs like Dublin or Rangers, and clubs like Apollo. There are also a few after hours in Juffair.

Amwaj island has a few sports bars, pubs and clubs. Cellar 59 located at Rotana Hotel is the club to go to if you don´t fancy driving to town. There is another branch of Lanters also serving soof, drinks and hosting happy hours and life music.

Hotels like Four Seasons or Ritz Carlton often host very chic and trendy parties for the most selected crowd.

48.TREE OF LIFE

Your visit to Bahrain wont be completed until you visit the Tree of life. This tree is over 400 years old and its situated in the middle of the dessert, about 40 km driving from Manama. What makes this tree so special? The fact that it is isolated in the middle of the dessert, and still displaying beautifully green leafs. How this tree survive is a mystery.

49. WILDLIFE

Al Areen Wildlife Park and Reserve is the home to the wildlife in the Kingdom. Is the only park in the region where species live in a natural and protected environment. This reserve is located in AlMarkh, five kilometers south-west of Jabal AlDukhan, two kilometers from the Zallaq shoreline.

Take a bus tour along the park to see the animals living in their natural habitat. Cgheck their website http://www.alareen.org/ fro more information.

50. WATCH SOME RUGBY

Bahrain RFC is the 2018 champion of the East Asia Cup. Needless to say that rugby is big in the country. Head to Bahrain Rugby Club on a Match day to see the team in action. You can also visit the club as a guest of a member. If you are military personnel or member of other rugby club you can enter the club without the need of a member.

BONUS. USEFUL WORDS

Shukran = Thank you.

Khalas = enough

Maa Salaama- Goodbye

Habibi- My love, used in a friendly way, very casual

Insha'Allah- God willing

Mash'Allah- Used to say something is pretty/nice

Yalla- Let's go/c'mon/ hurry up

>TOURIST

BONUS BOOK

50 THINGS TO KNOW ABOUT PACKING LIGHT FOR TRAVEL

PACK THE RIGHT WAY EVERY TIME

AUTHOR: MANIDIPA BHATTACHARYYA

Edited by Melanie Howthorne

ABOUT THE AUTHOR

Manidipa Bhattacharyya is a creative writer and editor, with an
education in English literature and Linguistics. After working in the IT
industry for seven long years she decided to call it quits and follow her
heart instead. Manidipa has been ghost writing, editing, proof reading
and doing secondary research services for many story tellers and article
writers for about three years. She stays in Kolkata, India with her
husband and a busy two year old. In her own time Manidipa enjoys
travelling, photography and writing flash fiction.

Manidipa believes in travelling light and never carries anything that she
couldn't haul herself on a trip. However, travelling with her child
changed the scenario. She seemed to carry the entire world with her for
the baby on the first two trips. But good sense prevailed and she is
again working her way to becoming a light traveler, this time with a
kid.

INTRODUCTION

*He who would travel happily
must travel light.*

-Antoine de Saint-Exupéry

Travel takes you to different places from seas and
mountains to deserts and much more. In your travels
you get to interact with different people and their
cultures. You will, however, enjoy the sights and
interact positively with these new people even more,
if you are travelling light.

When you travel light your mind can be free from
worry about your belongings. You do not have to
spend precious vacation time waiting for your
luggage to arrive after a long flight. There is be no
chance of your bags going missing and the best part is
that you need not pay a fee for checked baggage.

People who have mastered this art of packing light
will root for you to take only one carry-on, wherever
you go. However, many people can find it really hard
to pack light. More so if you are travelling with
children. Differentiating between "must have" and
"just in case" items is the starting point. There will be
ample shopping avenues at your destination which are
just waiting to be explored.

This book will show you 'packing' in a new 'light' – pun intended – and help you to embrace light packing practices for all of your future travels.

Off to packing!

DEDICATION

I dedicate this book to all the travel buffs that I know, who have given me great insights into the contents of their backpacks.

THE RIGHT TRAVEL GEAR

1. CHOOSE YOUR TRAVEL GEAR CAREFULLY

While selecting your travel gear, pick items that are light weight, durable and most importantly, easy to carry. There are cases with wheels so you can drag them along – these are usually on the heavy side because of the trolley. Alternatively a backpack that you can carry comfortably on your back, or even a duffel bag that you can carry easily by hand or sling across your body are also great options. Whatever you choose, one thing to keep in mind is that the luggage itself should not weigh a ton, this will give you the flexibility to bring along one extra pair of shoes if you so desire.

2. CARRY THE MINIMUM NUMBER OF BAGS

Selecting light weight luggage is not everything. You need to restrict the number of bags you carry as well. One carry-on size bag is ideal for light travel. Most carriers allow one cabin baggage plus one purse, handbag or camera bag as long as it slides under the seat in front. So technically, you can carry two items of luggage without checking them in.

3. PACK ONE EXTRA BAG

Always pack one extra empty bag along with your essential items. This could be a very light weight duffel bag or even a sturdy tote bag which takes up minimal space. In the event that you end up buying a lot of souvenirs, you already have a handy bag to stuff all that into and do not have to spend time hunting for an appropriate bag.

I'm very strict with my packing and have everything in its right place. I never change a rule. I hardly use anything in the hotel room. I wheel my own wardrobe in and that's it.

Charlie Watts

CLOTHES & ACCESSORIES

4. PLAN AHEAD

Figure out in advance what you plan to do on your trip. That will help you to pick that one dress you need for the occasion. If you are going to attend a wedding then you have to carry formal wear. If not, you can ditch the gown for something lighter that will be comfortable during long walks or on the beach.

5. WEAR THAT JACKET

Remember that wearing items will not add extra luggage for your air travel. So wear that bulky jacket that you plan to carry for your trip. This saves space and can also help keep you warm during the chilly flight.

6. MIX AND MATCH

Carry clothes that can be interchangeably used to reinvent your look. Find one top that goes well with a couple of pairs of pants or skirts. Use tops, shirts and jackets wisely along with other accessories like a scarf or a stole to create a new look.

7. CHOOSE YOUR FABRIC WISELY

Stuffing clothes in cramped bags definitely takes its toll which results in wrinkles. It is best to carry wrinkle free, synthetic clothes or merino tops. This will eliminate the need for that small iron you usually bring along.

8. DITCH CLOTHES PACK UNDERWEAR

Pack more underwear and socks. These are the things that will give you a fresh feel even if you do not get a chance to wear fresh clothes. Moreover these are easy to wash and can be dried inside the hotel room itself.

9. CHOOSE DARK OVER LIGHT

While picking your clothes choose dark coloured ones. They are easy to colour coordinate and can last longer before needing a wash. Accidental food spills and dirt from the road are less visible on darker clothes.

10. WEAR YOUR JEANS

Take only one pair of Jeans with you, which you should wear on the flight. Remember to pick a pair that can be worn for sightseeing trips and is equally eloquent for dinner. You can add variety by adding light weight cargoes and chinos.

11. CARRY SMART ACCESSORIES

The right accessory can give you a fresh look even with the same old dress. An intelligent neck-piece, a couple of bright scarves, stoles or a sarong can be used in a number of ways to add variety to your clothing. These light weight beauties can double up as a nursing cover, a light blanket, beach wear, a modesty cover for visiting places of worship, and also makes for an enthralling game of peek-a-boo.

12. LEARN TO FOLD YOUR GARMENTS

Seasoned travellers all swear by rolling their clothes for compact and wrinkle free packing. Bundle packing, where you roll the clothes around a central object as if tying it up, is also a popular method of compact and wrinkle free packing. Stacking folded clothes one on top of another is a big no-no as it makes creases extreme and they are difficult to get rid of without ironing.

13. WASH YOUR DIRTY LAUNDRY

One of the ways to avoid carrying loads of clothes is to wash the clothes you carry. At some places you might get to use the laundry services or a Laundromat but if you are in a pinch, best solution is to wash them yourself. If that is the plan then carrying quick drying clothes is highly recommended, which most often also happen to be the wrinkle free variety.

14. LEAVE THOSE TOWELS BEHIND

Regular towels take up a lot of space, are heavy and take ages to dry out. If you are staying at hotels they will provide you with towels anyway. If you are travelling to a remote place, where the availability of towels look doubtful, carry a light weight travel towel of viscose material to do the job.

15. USE A COMPRESSION BAG

Compression bags are getting lots of recommendation now days from regular travellers. These are useful for saving space in your luggage when you have to pack bulky dresses. While packing for the return trip, get help from the hotel staff to arrange a vacuum cleaner.

FOOTWEAR

16. PUT ON YOUR HIKING BOOTS

If you have plans to go hiking or trekking during your trip, you will need those bulky hiking boots. The best way to carry them is to wear them on flight to save space and luggage weight. You can remove the boots once inside and be comfortable in your socks.

17. PICKING THE RIGHT SHOES

Shoes are often the bulkiest items, along with being the dainty if you are a female. They need care and take up a lot of space in your luggage. It is advisable therefore to pick shoes very carefully. If you plan to do a lot of walking and site seeing, then wearing a pair of comfortable walking shoes are a must. For more formal occasions you can carry durable, light weight flats which will not take up much space.

18. STUFF SHOES

If you happen to pack a pair of shoes, ensure you utilize their hollow insides. Tuck small items like rolled up socks or belts to save space. They will also be easy to find.

TOILETRIES

19. STASHING TOILETRIES

Carry only absolute necessities. Airline rules dictate that for one carry-on bag, liquids and gels must be in 3.4 ounce (100ml) bottles or less, and must be packed in a one quart zip-lock bag. If you are planning to stay in a hotel, the basic things will be provided for you. It's best is to buy the rest from the local market at your destination.

20. TAKE ALONG TAMPONS

Tampons are a hard to find item in a lot of countries. Figure out how many you need and pack accordingly. For longer stays you can buy them online and have them delivered to where you are staying.

21. GET PAMPERED BEFORE YOU TRAVEL

Some avid travellers suggest getting a pedicure and manicure just the day before travelling. This not only gives you a well kept look, you also save the trouble of packing nail polish. Remember, every little bit of weight reduced adds up.

ELECTRONICS

22. LUGGING ALONG ELECTRONICS

Electronics have a large role to play in our lives today. Most of us cannot imagine our lives away from our phones, laptops or tablets. However while travelling, one must consider the amount of weight these electronics add to our luggage. Thankfully smart phones come along with all the essentials tools like a camera, email access, picture editing tools and more. They are smart to the point of eliminating the need to carry multiple gadgets. Choose a smart phone that suits all your requirements and travel with the world in your palms or pocket.

23. REDUCE THE NUMBER OF CHARGERS

If you do travel with multiple electronic devices, you will have to bear the additional burden of carrying all their chargers too. Check if a single charger can be used for multiple devices. You might also consider investing in a pocket charger. These small devices support multiple devices while keeping you charged on the go.

24. TRAVEL FRIENDLY APPS

Along with smart phones come numerous apps, which are immensely helpful in our travels. You name it and you have an app for it at hand – take pictures, sharing with friends and family, torch to light dark roads, maps, checking flight/train times, find hotels and many other things. Use these smart alternatives to traditional items like books to eliminate weight and save space.

I get ideas about what's essential when packing my suitcase.

-Diane von Furstenberg

TRAVELLING WITH KIDS

25. BRING ALONG THE STROLLER

Kids might enjoy walking for a while but they soon tire out and a stroller is the just the right thing for them to rest in while you continue your tour. Strollers also double duty as a luggage carrier and shopping bag holder. Remember to pick a light weight, easy to handle brand of stroller. Better yet, find out in advance if you can rent a stroller at your destination.

26. BRING ONLY ENOUGH DIAPERS FOR YOUR TRIP

Diapers take up a lot of space and add to the weight of your luggage. Therefore it is advisable to carry just enough diapers to last through the trip and a few for afterwards, till you buy fresh stock at your destination. Unless of course you are travelling to a really remote area, in which case you have no choice but to carry the load. Otherwise diapers are something you will find pretty easily.

27. TAKE ONLY A COUPLE OF TOYS

Children are easily attracted by new things in their environment. While travelling they will find numerous 'new' objects to scrutinize and play with. Packing just one favorite toy is enough, or if there is no favorite toy leave out all of them in favor of stories or imaginary games.

28. CARRY KID FRIENDLY SNACKS

Create a small snack counter in your bag to store away quick bites for those sudden hunger pangs. Depending on the child's age this could include chocolates, raisins, dry fruits, granola bars or biscuits. Also keep a bottle of water handy for your little one.

These things do not add much weight and can be adjusted in a handbag or knapsack.

29. GAMES TO CARRY

Create some travel specific, imaginary games if you have slightly grown up children, like spot the attractions. Keep a coloring book and colors handy for in-flight or hotel time. Apps on your smart phone can keep the children engaged with cartoons and story books. Older children are often entertained by games available on phones or tablets. This cuts the weight of luggage down while keeping the kids entertained.

30. LET THE KIDS CARRY THEIR LOAD

A good thing is to start early sharing of responsibilities. Let your child pick a bag of his or her choice and pack it themselves. Keep tabs on what they are stuffing in their bags by asking if they will be using that item on the trip. It could start out being just an entertainment bag initially but with growing years they will learn to sort the useful from the superfluous. Children as little as four can maneuver a small trolley suitcase like a pro- their experience in pull along toys credit. If you are worried that you may be pulling it for them, you may want to start with a backpack.

31. DECIDE ON LOCATION FOR CHILDREN TO SLEEP

While on a trip you might not always get a crib at your destination, and carrying one will make life all the more difficult. Instead call ahead to see if there are any cribs or roll out beds for children. You may even put blankets on the floor. Weave them a story about camping and they will gladly sleep without any trouble.

32. GET BABY PRODUCTS DELIVERED AT YOUR DESTINATION

If you are absolutely paranoid about not getting your favourite variety of diaper or brand of baby food, check out online stores like amazon.com for services in your destination city. You can buy things online ahead of your travel and get them delivered to your hotel upon arrival.

33. FEEDING NEEDS OF YOUR INFANTS

If you are travelling with a breastfed infant, you save the trouble of carrying bottles and bottle sanitization kits. For special food, or medications, you may need to call ahead to make sure you have a refrigerator where you are staying.

34. FEEDING NEEDS OF YOUR TODDLER

With the progression from infancy to toddler, their dietary requirements too evolve. You will have to pack some snacks for travelling time. Fresh fruits and vegetables can be purchased at your destination. Most of the cities you travel to in whichever part of the world, will have baby food products and formulas, available at the local drug-store or the supermarket.

35. PICKING CLOTHES FOR YOUR BABY

Contrary to popular belief, babies can do without many changes of clothes. At the most pack 2 outfits per day. Pack mix and match type clothes for your little one as well. Pick things which are comfortable to wear and quick to dry.

36. SELECTING SHOES FOR YOUR BABY

Like outfits, kids can make do with two pairs of comfortable shoes. If you can get some water resistant shoes it will be best. To expedite drying wet shoes, you can stuff newspaper in them then wrap them with newspaper and leave them to dry overnight.

37. KEEP ONE CHANGE OF CLOTHES HANDY

Travelling with kids can be tricky. Keep a change of clothes for the kids and mum handy in your purse or tote bag. This takes a bit of space in your hand luggage but comes extremely handy in case there are any accidents or spills.

38. LEAVE BEHIND BABY ACCESSORIES

Baby accessories like their bed, bath tub, car seat, crib etc. should be left at home. Many hotels provide a crib on request, while car seats can be borrowed from friends or rented. Babies can be given a bath in the hotel sink or even in the adult bath tub with a little bit of water. If you bring a few bath toys, they can be used in the bath, pool, and out of water. They can also be sanitized easily in the sink.

39. CARRY A SMALL LOAD OF PLASTIC BAGS

With children around there are chances of a number of soiled clothes and diapers. These plastic bags help to sort the dirt from the clean inside your big bag.

These are very light weight and come in handy to other carry stuff as well at times.

PACK WITH A PURPOSE

40. PACKING FOR BUSINESS TRIPS

One neutral-colored suit should suffice. It can be paired with different shirts, ties and accessories for different occasions. One pair of black suit pants could be worn with a matching jacket for the office or with a snazzy top for dinner.

41. PACKING FOR A CRUISE

Most cruises have formal dinners, and that formal dress usually takes up a lot of space. However you might find a tuxedo to rent. For women, a short black dress with multiple accessory options will do the trick.

42. PACKING FOR A LONG TRIP OVER DIFFERENT CLIMATES

The secret packing mantra for travel over multiple climates is layering. Layering traps air around your body creating insulation against the cold. The same light t-shirt that is comfortable in a warmer climate can be the innermost layer in a colder climate.

REDUCE SOME MORE WEIGHT

43. LEAVE PRECIOUS THINGS AT HOME

Things that you would hate to lose or get damaged leave them at home. Precious jewelry, expensive gadgets or dresses, could be anything. You will not require these on your trip. Leave them at home and spare the load on your mind.

44. SEND SOUVENIRS BY MAIL

If you have spent all your money on purchasing souvenirs, carrying them back in the same bag that you brought along would be difficult. Either pack everything in another bag and check it in the airport or get everything shipped to your home. Use an international carrier for a secure transit, but this could be more expensive than the checking fees at the airport.

45. AVOID CARRYING BOOKS

Books equal to weight. There are many reading apps which you can download on your smart phone or tab.

Plus there are gadgets like Kindle and Nook that are thinner and lighter alternatives to your regular book.

CHECK, GET, SET, CHECK AGAIN

46. STRATEGIZE BEFORE PACKING

Create a travel list and prepare all that you think you need to carry along. Keep everything on your bed or floor before packing and then think through once again – do I really need that? Any item that meets this question can be avoided. Remove whatever you don't really need and pack the rest.

47. TEST YOUR LUGGAGE

Once you have fully packed for the trip take a test trip with your luggage. Take your bags and go to town for window shopping for an hour. If you enjoy your hour long trip it is good to go, if not, go home and reduce the load some more. Repeat this test till you hit the right weight.

48. ADD A ROLL OF DUCT TAPE

You might wonder why, when this book has been talking about reducing stuff, we're suddenly asking

95

you to pack something totally unusual. This is
because when you have limited supplies, duct tape is
immensely helpful for small repairs – a broken bag,
leaking zip-lock bag, broken sunglasses, you name it
and duct tape can fix it, temporarily.

49. LIST OF ESSENTIAL ITEMS

Even though the emphasis is on packing light, there
are things which have to be carried for any trip. Here
is our list of essentials:

•Passport/Visa or any other ID

•Any other paper work that might be required on a trip
  like permits, hotel reservation confirmations etc.

•Medicines – all your prescription medicines and
  emergency kit, especially if you are travelling with
  children

•Medical or vaccination records

•Money in foreign currency if travelling to a different
  country

•Tickets- Email or Message them to your phone

50. MAKE THE MOST OF YOUR TRIP

Wherever you are going, whatever you hope to do we encourage you to embrace it whole-heartedly. Take in the scenery, the culture and above all, enjoy your time away from home.

On a long journey even a straw weighs heavy.

-Spanish Proverb

PACKING AND PLANNING TIPS

A Week before Leaving

- Arrange for someone to take care of pets and water plants.

- Stop mail and newspaper.

- Notify Credit Card companies where you are going.

- Change your thermostat settings.

- Car inspected, oil is changed, and tires have the correct pressure.

- Passports and photo identification is up to date.

- Pay bills.

- Copy important items and download travel Apps.

- Start collecting small bills for tips.

Right Before Leaving

- Clean out refrigerator.

- Empty garbage cans.

- Lock windows.

- Make sure you have the proper identification with you.

- Bring cash for tips.

- Remember travel documents.

- Lock door behind you.

- Remember wallet.

- Unplug items in house and pack chargers.

READ OTHER
GREATER THAN A TOURIST
BOOKS

Greater Than a Tourist San Miguel de Allende Guanajuato Mexico:
50 Travel Tips from a Local by Tom Peterson

Greater Than a Tourist – Lake George Area New York USA:
50 Travel Tips from a Local by Janine Hirschklau

Greater Than a Tourist – Monterey California United States:
50 Travel Tips from a Local by Katie Begley

Greater Than a Tourist – Chanai Crete Greece:
50 Travel Tips from a Local by Dimitra Papagrigoraki

Greater Than a Tourist – The Garden Route Western Cape Province
South Africa: 50 Travel Tips from a Local by Li-Anne McGregor van
Aardt

Greater Than a Tourist – Sevilla Andalusia Spain:
50 Travel Tips from a Local by Gabi Gazon

Greater Than a Tourist – Kota Bharu Kelantan Malaysia:
50 Travel Tips from a Local by Aditi Shukla

Children's Book: Charlie the Cavalier Travels the World by Lisa
Rusczyk

> TOURIST

Visit Greater Than a Tourist for Free Travel Tips
   http://GreaterThanATourist.com

Sign up for the Greater Than a Tourist Newsletter for
   discount days, new books, and travel information:
   http://eepurl.com/cxspyf

Follow us on Facebook for tips, images, and ideas:
   https://www.facebook.com/GreaterThanATourist

Follow us on Pinterest for travel tips and ideas:
   http://pinterest.com/GreaterThanATourist

Follow us on Instagram for beautiful travel images:
   http://Instagram.com/GreaterThanATourist

> TOURIST

Please leave your honest review of this book on Amazon and Goodreads. Please send your feedback to GreaterThanaTourist@gmail.com as we continue to improve the series. We appreciate your positive and constructive feedback. Thank you.

METRIC CONVERSIONS

TEMPERATURE

110° F — — 40° C
100° F —
90° F — — 30° C
80° F —
70° F — — 20° C
60° F —
50° F — — 10° C
40° F —
32° F — — 0° C
20° F —
10° F — — -10° C
0° F —
-10° F — — -18° C
-20° F — — -30° C

To convert F to C:

Subtract 32, and then multiply by 5/9 or .5555.

To Convert C to F:
Multiply by 1.8 and then add 32.

32F = 0C

LIQUID VOLUME

To Convert:..................Multiply by
U.S. Gallons to Liters................ 3.8
U.S. Liters to Gallons 26
Imperial Gallons to U.S. Gallons 1.2
Imperial Gallons to Liters....... 4.55
Liters to Imperial Gallons 22
1 Liter = .26 U.S. Gallon
1 U.S. Gallon = 3.8 Liters

DISTANCE

To convert ....Multiply by
Inches to Centimeters 2.54
Centimeters to Inches 39
Feet to Meters...................... .3
Meters to Feet 3.28
Yards to Meters 91
Meters to Yards 1.09
Miles to Kilometers 1.61
Kilometers to Miles............ .62
1 Mile = 1.6 km
1 km = .62 Miles

WEIGHT

1 Ounce = .28 Grams
1 Pound = .4555 Kilograms
1 Gram = .04 Ounce
1 Kilogram = 2.2 Pounds

TRAVEL QUESTIONS

- Do you bring presents home to family or friends after a vacation?

- Do you get motion sick?

- Do you have a favorite billboard?

- Do you know what to do if there is a flat tire?

- Do you like a sun roof open?

- Do you like to eat in the car?

- Do you like to wear sun glasses in the car?

- Do you like toppings on your ice cream?

- Do you use public bathrooms?

- Did you bring your cell phone and does it have power?

- Do you have a form of identification with you?

- Have you ever been pulled over by a cop?

- Have you ever given money to a stranger on a road trip?

- Have you ever taken a road trip with animals?

- Have you ever went on a vacation alone?

- Have you ever run out of gas?

- If you could move to any place in the world, where would it be?

- If you could travel anywhere in the world, where would you travel?

- If you could travel in any vehicle, which one would it be?

- If you had three things to wish for from a magic genie, what would they be?

- If you have a driver's license, how many times did it take you to pass the test?

- What are you the most afraid of on vacation?

- What do you want to get away from the most when you are on vacation?

- What foods smells bad to you?

- What item do you bring on ever trip with you away from home?

- What makes you sleepy?

- What song would you love to hear on the radio when you're cruising on the highway?

- What travel job would you want the least?

- What will you miss most while you are away from home?

- What is something you always wanted to try?

- What is the best road side attraction that you ever saw?

- What is the farthest distance you ever biked?

- What is the farthest distance you ever walked?

- What is the weirdest thing you needed to buy while on vacation?

- What is your favorite candy?

- What is your favorite color car?

- What is your favorite family vacation?

- What is your favorite food?

- What is your favorite gas station drink or food?

- What is your favorite license plate design?

- What is your favorite restaurant?

- What is your favorite smell?

- What is your favorite song?

- What is your favorite sound that nature makes?

- What is your favorite thing to bring home from a vacation?

- What is your favorite vacation with friends?

- What is your favorite way to relax?

- Where is the farthest place you ever traveled in a car?

- Where is the farthest place you ever went North, South, East and West?

- Where is your favorite place in the world?

- Who is your favorite singer?

- Who taught you how to drive?

- Who will you miss the most while you are away?

- Who if the first person you will contact when you get to your destination?

- Who brought you on your first vacation?

- Who likes to travel the most in your life?

- Would you rather be hot or cold?

- Would you rather drive above, below, or at the speed limited?

- Would you rather drive on a highway or a back road?

- Would you rather go on a train or a boat?

- Would you rather go to the beach or the woods?

TRAVEL BUCKET LIST

1.

2.

3.

4.

5.

6.

7.

8.

9.

10.

NOTES

Made in the USA
San Bernardino, CA
22 March 2019